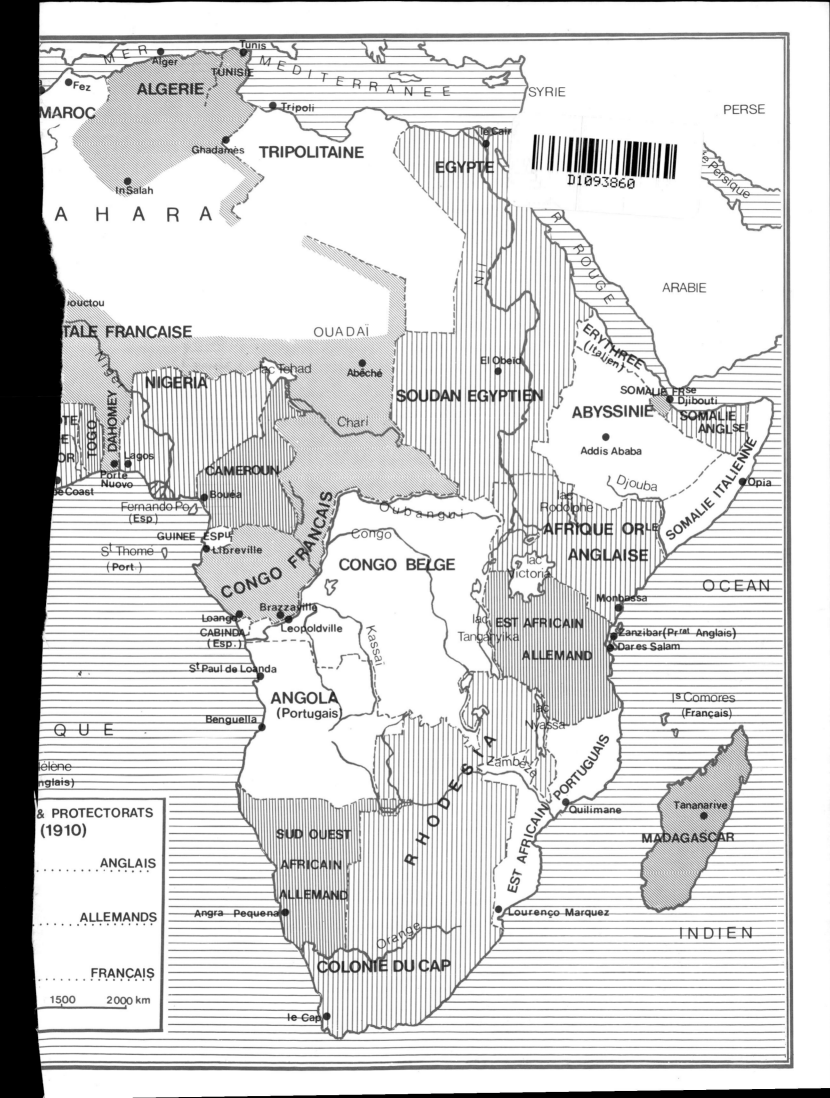

SOUTH AFRICA BLACK AFRICA

1890 – 1925

AFRICA 1900

A CONTINENT EMERGES

A HISTORY IN DOCUMENTARY PHOTOGRAPHS
BY
ERIC BASCHET

CONTENTS

5

AFRICA DISCOVERS EUROPE

Africa lies today just a stone's throw from Europe. A few hours' flight and we are enthralled by its riches, its cultures and its contradictions. The dreams awakened by adventure novels and travel journals already belong to the past. The all to depressing, indeed tragic reality of Africa has gripped us and we are never the same again. Yet only about one and a half centuries ago René Caillié managed a feat which has been the talk of succeeding generations. Disguised as an Arab trader, he succeeded in reaching Timbuktu, one of the sacred cities of African Islam. He had broached a secret guarded for so long and now there were fewer blank spaces on the map. A dauntless explorer. Who would not grant him this accolade? Yet Caillié was not the first nor was he to be the last.

In antiquity a Pharao sent out an expedition under the auspices of the seafaring Phoenicians. The chronicles relate that the journey took three years. Even if the expedition really did take place, it can hardly be said to have enlarged our knowledge of the African continent. Later, a long time afterwards, the Arabs were to perform much greater deeds. They set out from the North African coasts for the interior of the continent and reached the southern Sahara, the Kingdom of Mali and Senegal. Among their number were missionaries as well as geographers and traders and they brought new believers to Islam. Chinese too appeared on the eastern coast of Africa who described the customs of the natives and took home with them a mythical beast, the giraffe. Still Africa remained a mysterious continent until well into the 15th century. Its geographical contours were unknown.

Men puzzled over the sources of its rivers, in particular that of the celebrated Nile. In European legend the Kingdom of John awaited far away in the East the arrival of the Christians. To make a long story short, Africa lived on, remote from what was going on elsewhere, preoccupied with its own concerns and split up into innumerable tribes. Only a few of these were consolidated for a brief period by ambitious conquerors. It was indeed the Age of Isolation.

The Portuguese were the first Europeans to penetrate this remote fastness. The first Portuguese explorers set off to find a sea route to India. They were amazed by one thing after another. While they were sailing along the West Coast of Africa, they encountered a unknown world. They crossed the Equator to reach the Mouth of the Congo. In 1487 Bartholomew Diaz had a curious adventure. The coast still lay to port but his ship was sailing north. Diaz has passed the Cape of Storms, which was soon to be renamed the Cape of Good Hope. India now lay open to Europe. Africa too, but it was to take longer before the Europeans grasped the fact. The French and English followed close on the heels of the Portuguese and established trading centres in the Golf of Guinea. And in 1652 the Dutch managed to establish a permanent post at the Cape. The Portuguese established themselves in Angola and Mozambique. The Europeans and the Arabs entered on profitable trade with the natives. Black slaves were exchanged for weapons, spirits, tobacco and material. But all this trade was limited to the coasts. The interior was yet to be colonized. The slave trade had already shattered Africa's political order.

States arose or fell into decline. Kings and chieftains grew rich on the lucrative bargains they drove with the slave traders. Africa began indeed to change.

It was to change still more in the 19th century. Its inner borders, its way of life, the sovereignty of its states were no longer as they had been. The Europeans had ceased to buy men and women. The slave trade fell into decline. Slavery was abolished in the British Empire in 1833, in 1848 in the French colonies and in 1865 in the United States of America. But explorers' appetite for knowledge was insatiable. Africa was systematically explored. The German explorer Barth crossed Chad and the Niger valleys. His compatriot, Nachtigal, was interested in Togo and the Cameroons. Duveyrier, Flatters, Charles de Foucauld, Faidherbe, Gallienie, Binger, Monteil... all these names are recalling the exploration of West Africa by the French, the march through the Sahara while Savorgnon de Brazza explored the Oguooe and the course of the Nile. The English must not be forgotten. The most famous of these is surely David Livingstone, the doctor and clergyman with such a passion for Africa. In 1840 he sat foot on the continent at the Cape and nine years later he crossed the Kalahari Desert. Then he explored the course of the Sambesi and reached Victoria Falls and Lake Nyasa. He described the magnificent scenery of East Africa to his compatriot and told of his fights against slave traders and of the spread of Christianity. Near Lake Taganyika he was seized by the desire to explore further. Europe lost all trace of Livingstone. In 1871 the American newspaper "The New York Herald Tribune" sent a reporter, John R. Stanley, to Africa. His task was to trace Livingstone and give his readers a detailed account of the great adventure. After many months of exploration Stanley succeeded.

Their meeting is commemorated by an inscription. On side is a relief of the journalist followed by his bearers and on the other the missionary. Stanley remarks to Livingstone "Livingstone, I presume?" British humour in the heart of Africa. Not long afterwards Stanley too was to become an African explorer. In the service of the Belgian King he contributed substantially to our knowledge of the Mouth of the Congo.

Scientific curiosity was not the only European motivation for exploring Africa. General Meynier writes that Barth's travels proved the existence of wide stretches of fertile land in the interior of Africa which were well deserving European notice. Jules Ferry puts it even more bluntly. He contends that colonial politics is the daughter of the Industrial Revolution. He adds unabashedly: "The superior races have certain rights over the inferior ones, rights devolving from duties. They have the duty of civilizing the inferior races." Most Europeans of that era thought and spoke in that vein. Rudyard Kipling's "the white man's burden" is out of the mould which produced Joseph Chamberlain's declaration that "The British race is the greatest master race the world has ever known." The fear of overpopulation, the search for raw materials and new markets, new possibilities of investing ready capital, the politics of national prestige, the machinations of diplomats: Europe inflicted its customs, its languages, its religions on the entire world and particularly on Africa. Between 1880 and 1895 Africa was finally conquered and partitioned among the colonial powers. Colonial empires emerged or enlarged their territory. The English domain stretched along the Cape to Cairo Railway. The French settled in West Africa and at the Mouth of the Congo. The Portuguese and Spanish consolidated their colonial possessions. Italy, Belgium and Germany emerged as colonial powers. Africa no longer belonged to the Africans. The Europe they got to know was the Europe of missionaries, of military and civilian administrators, settlers, all-conquering, imperialist and masterful pre–1914 Europe.

The Europe of this time was, moreover, a house divided. No sense of community guided the colonial powers. Instead daily rivalry occasionally led to wars. It is true that diplomatic efforts were made to reduce tensions. From November 1884 until February 1885 the Berlin Conference attempted to regulate shipping on the Niger and the Congo and ultimately recognized the independent Congo as a personal possession of King Leopold II. In subsequent years the great powers signed treaties determining the boundaries of their empires, borders which have survived decolonization itself. But in 1898 British and French troops stood face to face at Fashoda and in European capitals the public prepared for war. War did break out, but in a different place, in South Africa, where the Boers revolted against English domination. The descendants of Dutch settlers and French Huguenots, they believed that their pastoral way of life was in accordance with the will of God. They forcibly pushed back the Bantu in order to extend their grazing lands. Their justification for so doing was that the Bantu, conquerors in their turn, had driven out the Bushmen. When Great Britain took possession of the Cape Colony and abolished slavery there, the Boers set out their trek northwards. Recalling the Hebrews' passage out of Egypt, the Boers made their way to the Promised Land. The "Great Trek" took from 1834 to 1852. The Boers founded two republics, the Orange Free State and Transvaal, both recognized by Great Britain. The conflict had only apparently resolved; it had really just begun. Finds of gold and diamonds in Boer lands enticed adventurers. Financiers and speculators worked together and Cecil Rhodes plotted to incorporate both republics in the Crown possessions. After negotiations had led to concessions and ultimately to agreements, painstakingly detailed in treaties, which were subsequently broken, the war finally broke out in 1899. It lasted for three years and ended with a British victory. Transvaal and the Orange Free State were united to form the territory which was to become the Union of South Africa in 1910.

However, colonial rivalry in Africa was not yet at an end. The first world war affected the colonial empires, where fighting also erupted. The English and French fought against the Germans in the Cameroons, Togo and East Africa. In 1919 the German colonies were divided as spoils among the victors. And countless Africans fought in European armies and died in the trenches of Champagne and Picardy.

My enthusiasm for the Photos assembled here by Eric Baschet knows no bounds. The layman could hardly expect to find photographs of such a remarkable standard with regard to crispness and sharpness of details from plates made fifty or even eighty years ago. They never cease to amaze. Of course pictures of native African women carrying burdens on their heads, of rhinos shot on safari or of the great Africa's rivers are familiar from old geography books. Still the freshness of the photos in this volume never palls. The king of his wooden horse, the lips deformed beyond recognition, the appearance of European machinery ... These are not typical travel photos. Settlers and colonial administrators look as if they had sprung from the pages of a book of caricatures. These photos are more real than reality, documents of extraordinary aesthetic value.

Their historical value, too, should not be underestimated. This book is indeed a history in pictures of the impact of two worlds on one another. The one is at the zenith of power and renown. Seemingly nothing is unattainable. Machines, weapons and medical progress are its products. It believes firmly in the mission of bringing its civilisation, civilisation itself, to all men. The other world has not progressed for centuries. It admires Europe, opens its riches to it for exploitation, unaware that it too possesses superb art and its own ancient sources of wisdom, unaware of its uniqueness. The dependence of the one world on the other is a mirror image of the seeming superiority of the other. But these photos also shed the hard light of reality on the "benefits of civilization". The Europeans built schools to teach the Africans how to read and write. Vaccination and health care saved a great many lives. The introduction of modern agriculture fostered modest economic development. Whether one regrets or welcomes the impact of the two worlds on each other,

positive impulses must be said to have resulted from it. This sophisticated view of history is conveyed by Eric Baschet.

In addition, he shows us that Africa's history has been inextricably intertwined for a century with that of Europe. Neither Asia nor America have been interested in Africa until very recently. Yet the fact that African nations speak French, English, Spanish or Portuguese reveals the cultural bond between Europe and Africa. Thus Africans have come into contact with modern civilization, even when as Mohammedans or animists some can hardly be said to have been exposed to European religious influence. Today, at the close of decolonization, which had led to the emergence of independent African nations, this no longer means bondage. It is an unending dialogue. Oppression and conflict have ultimately given way to understanding. One last word : European penetration of Africa cannot be explained purely as a consequence of the phenomenon of colonialism. It is an integral part of the discovery of the world. Asia, China, India, Arabia had all been discovered. By the end of the 19th century, Tibet and Mongolia had revealed their secrets. Only the icecaps were left to explore. In 1909 explorers reached the North Pole, in 1911 the South Pole. The only blank spaces left on the map of the world were in Eastern Siberia, in New Guinea or in the Australian Outback. There was no mysterious continent left; the last blank spaces were soon to be coloured in. Looking through Eric Baschet's book, I am reminded of Paul Valéry's remark to the effect that the discovery of Africa was the dawn of "le temps du monde fini".

André KASPI
Lecturer at the
University of Lille II

BLACK-AFRICA

1900 - Winds of change were sweeping over Africa. It took the Marabu on the Nile by surprise and caught up with medicine men on the Congo as well as the Boers at the Cape of Good Hope. It was the breath of the 20th century, the breath of Europe itself.

CUSTOMS
AND TRADITIONS

The first surprise: Africa is a giant continent sprawling over 38 millions square kilometres. Even its fig trees measure up to 170m in diameter.

Its waterfalls can be over 100m in height like this one near Umtata in the Cape Colony, which reaches a height of 115m. Man is dwarfed by such wonders.

16

This village of wattle and adobe huts south of Lake Chad in Masai territory looks like an apiary.
There is a small "hut" next to each "dwelling" that is used as a millet granary.
It is build rather high to protect grain from dampness and rodents. In northern Cameroon dwellings can be entered by
ladder.

A chieftain in front of straw huts in northern Cameroon.

Dudmurah, a sultan of the Gadai, graciously allows his wives to wait on him.

A Masai beauty adored with bronze necklace and bracelets.

Washamba in front of their dwellings in East Africa.

Clay architecture. Is not this fortified mosque in the Sudan a match for Europe's cathedrals?

Native art in Tessaoua: A crocodile deity and village scenes.

Fetishes of the former Kings of Abomey in the Palace of Béhanguin. Some of them are over 400 years old.

A palace façade ornamented with simple geometric patterns. This is the harem of the Sultan of Tessaoua in Nigeria.

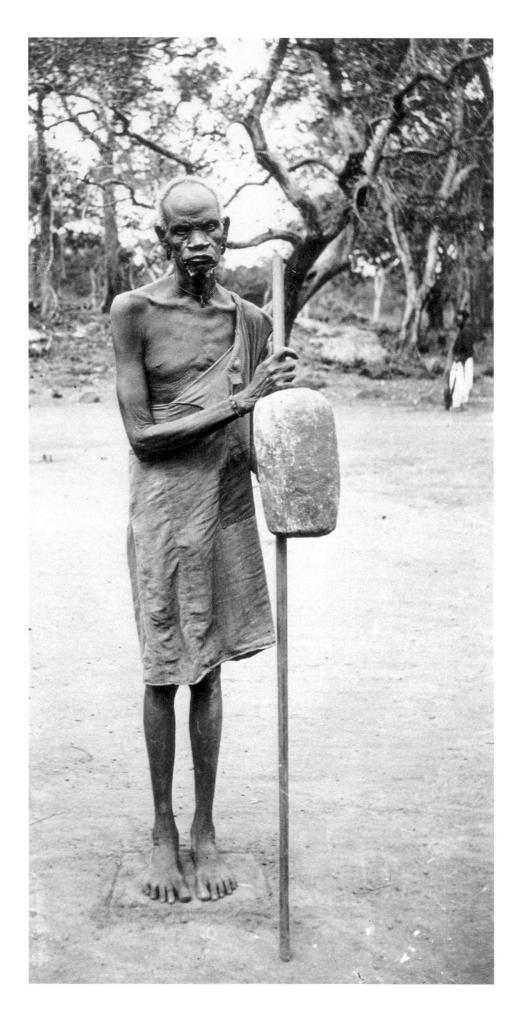

The old wise man, the proud young chieftain and the warrior. The mysterious language of clothing and facial expression has not changed at all.

*Grace, beauty and strength are combined in the Masai,
one of the most splendid races native to African soil.*

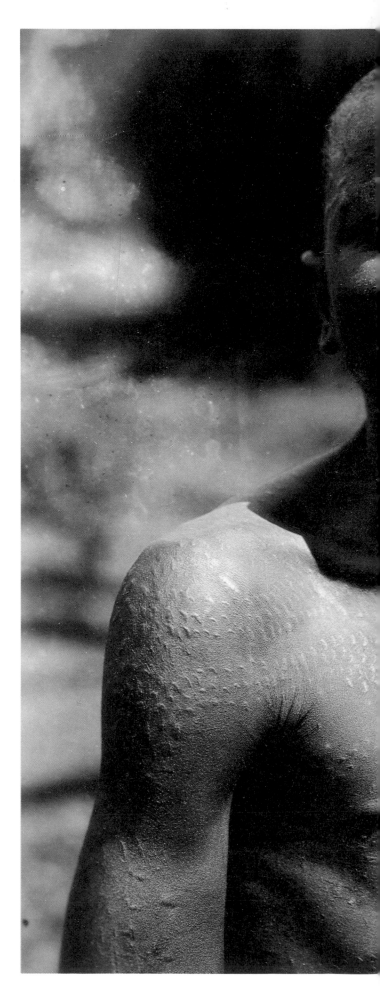

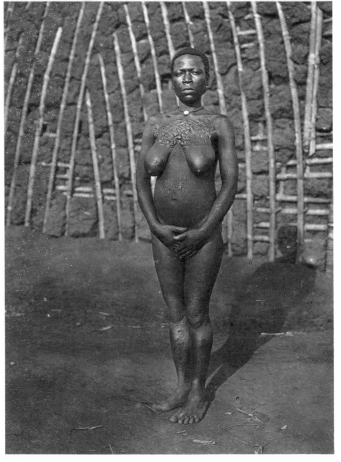

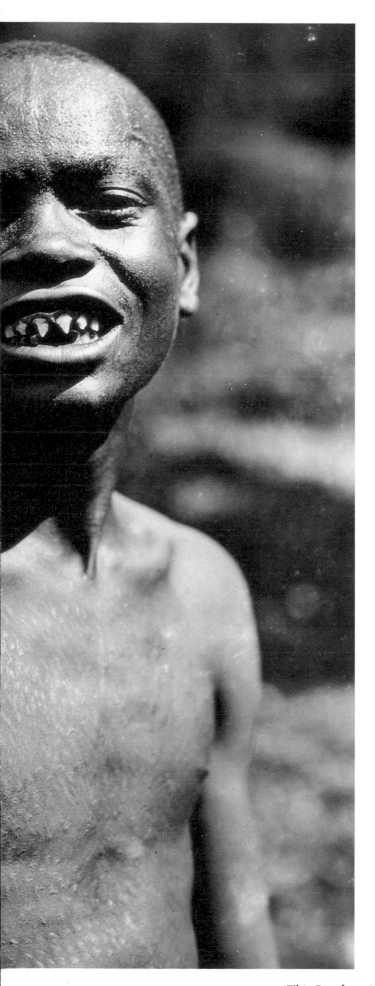

This Banda, with teeth filed to points, a cannibal from the Equatorial jungle, is a sharp contrast to the peaceful and civilized tribes of the Cameroons.

A classic procession: Water carriers on the Nile.

Fishing on the Niger.
In their floating calabashes women harvest the fish which have become entangled in the mesh of free-floating grass nets.

Two heron men in the Sudan.
In order to deceive the fish and thus harpoon them more easily with their long spears they imitate the cautious posture of the birds on stilts.

Women on the Niger bring in a huge dragnet in which fish have been caught over night.

A graceful fishing flotilla in Chad.
Each dugout contains a oarsman and a fisherman. Fish are caught in a three-cornered net which is fastened to two poles.

The only way through the dense jungle is by water.

Wild laughter echoes through the jungle. A hippopotamus puts on an aquashow in the Congo.

Apes in the treetops accompany the hunt with their shrill chattering.

Harvesters of wild honey, insensitive to beestings, climb giant trees in Abyssinia to collect the sweet liquid.

Armed with bows and arrows, spears and knives, an entire tribe goes lion hunting.

The crocodiles are baited with a dead goat. When one is caught
and killed, its stomach is slit open and the intact goat removed.

Five crocodiles, the impressive bag of an Sudanese tribe.

A crocodile is brought to a village by camel.
Here we see crocodile on the spit, a great delicacy. Crocodiles are said to taste of fish.

A hippopotamus is brought to the shore of the blue Nile to be gutted.

Two boys have killed this magnificent boa constrictor by surprising it in a deep postprandial sleep.

On the Upper Nile a spotted hyena has killed a young African.
But revenge is quick. Laid low by a spear the hyena is carried in triumph to the village.

Singing and dancing about the village King Kong. An enormous gorilla has been captured.

Night scene in central Africa. The old chieftain is honoured by a procession bearing straw torches.

N'django, a kundi player, celebrates the beauty of a girl from the Chadean tribe of the M'Baye.

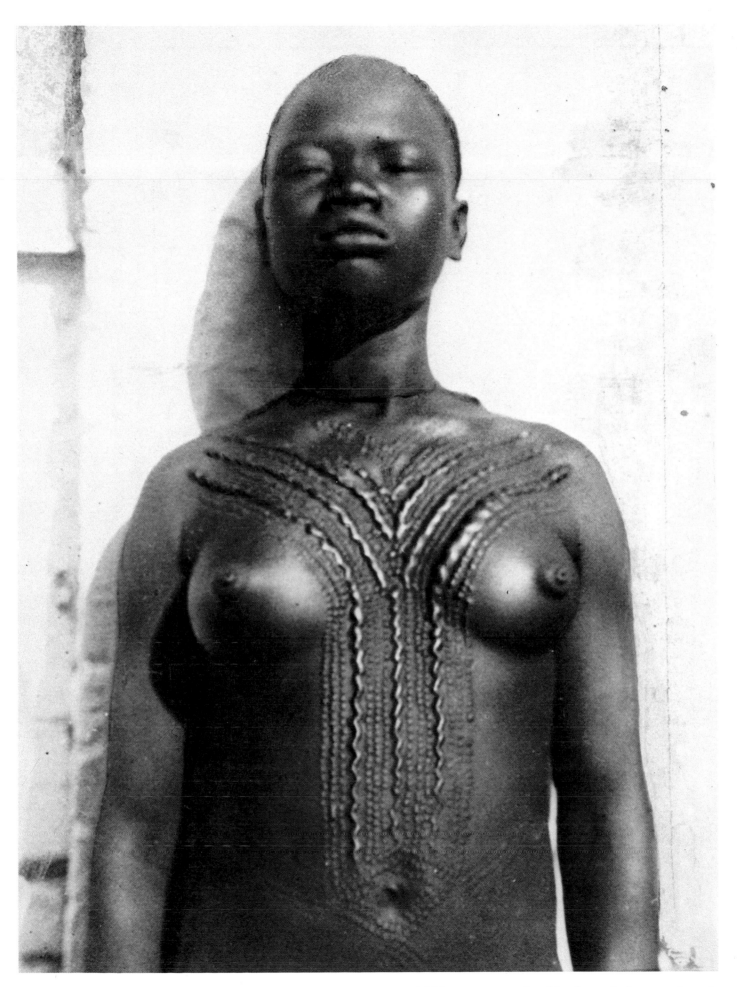

*Indelible patterns on the skin, formed of cuts and weals,
are regarded by both men and women as the most beautiful body ornament.*

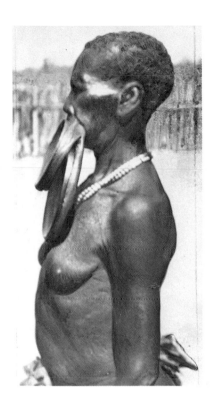

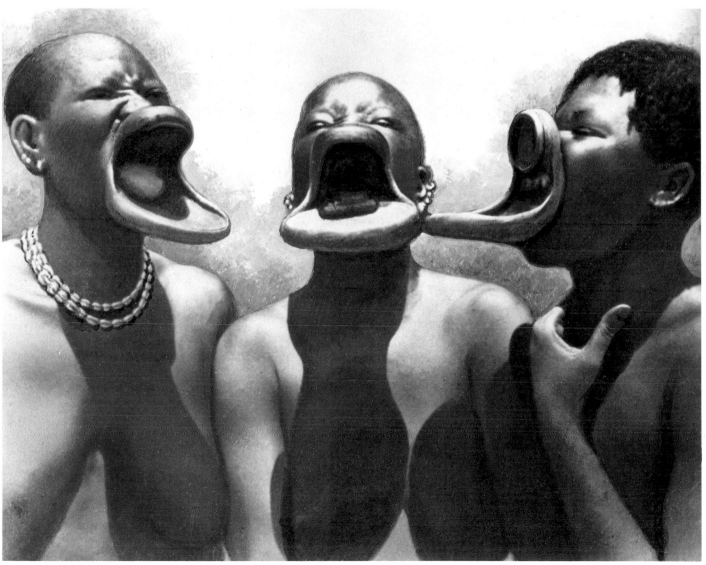

Although the "plate women" from the region south of Lake Chad can only babble, they are very talkative. With age the plates become even larger, the facial muscles grow limp and older women are no longer able to support the weight of their lips. But eating and drinking are difficult for young and old alike.

A simple life governed by rigid customs. Dancing, fishing, superstitious beliefs or waging war:
Tribal life consists of group activities in which each gesture is governed by ballet-like precision.

Back to the Middle Ages.
Everything is there: helmets and shirts of mail for the "knights"
and harness for the horses.

The armour of this warrior from the Niger dates back to the thirteenth century.
The warrior is followed by his "squire", a teller of tales and musician like the troubadours.

The retinue of King Rey Baiba, one of the great men of the Cameroons. Their uniforms were inspired by the armour of the Crusaders who were brought to Africa by Muslims from Palestine.

In the region of Lake Chad a man has died. His corpse is swathed in cotton bands, tied together by oxhide straps and dressed in a tunic. Then he is lowered into a narrow grave surmounted by a clay vessel.

Different burial customs prevail among the Madjia in Upper Shari. There the corpse is rubbed with oil and red wood dust before being lowered upright into a deep narrow square hole in the earth. A covering of leaves supposed to protect the corpse.

CUSTOMS AND TRADITIONS

When one crosses Africa from north to south, one encounters an incredible variety of races which can be divided roughly into two groups. On the one hand there are tribes converted by the Arabs to Islam, like the Tuareg on the Niger, the Haua in Chad or the splendid Songhai. The other group, south of the Ubangi-Shari, is made up of the fetish-worshipping tribes who have retained their original customs.

In the region of Bangui one encounters impenetrable equatorial jungle and the Sara, Bantu or Banda tribes. These cannibal tribes, their teeth filed to points, are clad in the simplest of raiment: leaves for the women, bark for the men. On holy days they deck themselves out in the loveliest of brightly coloured stones and rub their bodies with red ochre mixed with rancid oil. In their eyes, however, tattoos remained the most highly prized ornaments. Their dwellings are round holes in the earth, one metre in depth, which they cover over with bell-shaped structures of twigs and dried grass.

Further to the south in the jungle of the Congo dwell proud dwarf races who array themselves in feathers. There too is the home of the curious Mangbetu whose skulls are elongated at the back. To obtain this prized effect they bind cords round their heads from early childhood. Their profiles recall those of the ancient Egyptians. Great artisans possessing a profound feeling for harmonious proportion, the Mangbetu produce distinctive pottery, ivory carvings and basketry.

The dance, the form of expression common to all tribes, reaches choreographic heights among the Mangbetu. They also esteem the theatre and the cult of the stars. Their chieftain in particular, a despot, is under its spell. His numerous wives (like Ekibondo for instance he might have up to 63 wives) are accomodated in separate rooms. This is a prudent measure, and his male subjects are advised to avoid approaching them too closely.

Like the Egyptians the Mangbetu have subjugated another race, the Logos. Despite their athletic bodies of an unprepossessing appearance, the Logos are primarily animal breeders. Compared to this primitive race – and this explained their subjugation – the aristocratic Mangbetu seem highly cultured.

From the Lake District to the East Coast one finds pure races like the Masai with their coppery skin and almost Indian profiles only in a few remote areas today. Elsewhere the repeated onsloughts of conquerors, seafarers and slave traders have produced a racial mixture, even between Muslim and fetish-worshipping tribes.

The tsetse fly, all too often the scourge of domestic animals like the horse or the camel, halted the advances of Islam. But the European was not to be stopped and thus all the more prejudicial to the maintenance of native custom and tradition.

1900 – Two worlds collide. Which spirit, good or evil, is hidden in the camera?
Superstitious and suspicious, Africa makes overtures to 20th-century Europe. →

THE EUROPEANS ARRIVE

The French and English have a common goal, to cross Africa from east to west and to secure the upper reaches of the Nile for military and trading purposes. The English win the race. But Marchand's mission has not been in vain. His expedition from the Congo to the White Nile allows him to become friendly with the chieftains of the tribes whom he encounters on his travels.

No sooner have they learnt the rules of the game than the women of Fort Archam have a spirited go at "push ball".

This camera team too is about to capture contemporary life in Ubangi Shari for distant Europe.

With this gigantic telescopic lens the picture hunter is always on the lookout for curious flora and fauna.
Giraffe or Lobelia, elephant or giant heath? That is the question.

A detonation, a flash ... and the lioness is captured, if only on film. The "photo safari" is born. A calf is tied to a tree near a waterhole and the camera lens is trained on it, the shutter lens connected by a trip wire

to a magnesium flash. During the night the lioness trips the shutter. The whole series of photos is taken by repetition of this procedure. At last one can study beasts of prey in their natural habitat.

Rifle against trunk.
This huge elephant bull was shot at a distance of
20 metres before it had time to react.

A new passion: hunting in Africa. Achille Fould, one of the fathers of the modern safari.

Six o'clock p.m. A peacefully ruminating buffalo herd.
Suddenly the startled cry of a water bird. It has spied "firesticks" in the bush. Too late. The herd is decimated.

A photo of a hunting trophy.
With umbrella and pit helmet Henri de Rothschild is ensconced on his 536th bag, a hippopotamus.

Three future exhibits of the colonial exposition: a camel, a Sudanese crocodile and a lion.

Funeral ceremony for Tofta II, King of Porto Novo.
His bronze statue is in ceremonial garb.

Zumaou, King of the Dassa, is drawn by his ministers through the bush on a horse on wheels.

Two civilisations greet each other under a vast sunshade.
The Prince of Whales, the future Edward VIII, accepts the hommage of his new vassals on the Gold Coast.

King Ago-li-Agbo with members of his family in Nigeria. The Crown Prince, on his right, is responsible for municipal order under the Colonial Administration.

Ceremonial etiquette. Adjiki, son of Tofta II, presides as is his wont in the embroidered uniform of a French colonial administrator over a council of ministers, while on the Niger his people pays hommage to Marshal Franchet d'Espéry.

The main concern of the French is to teach the people how to read and write.

They instruct children as well as Senegalese sharpshooters.
During the Colonial Exposition in 1931 they found a "League for the Instruction of Illiterates".

*A further important task is to combat sleeping sickness, which is rampant in Equatorial Africa.
While scientists search for parasites under the microscope,*

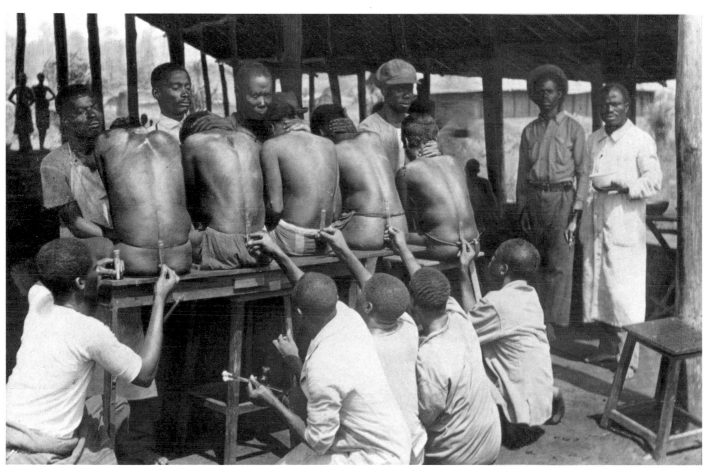

native nurses work at assembly-line pace taking blood samples and administering jabs in the buttocks.

French doctors train native nurses in flying schools and laboratories.

Not even the life and well-being of the animal kingdom is neglected,
as the case of a wounded marabu or of pelicans on the upper reaches of the Nile shows.

95

One must be prepared for anything and be able to bear any discomfort,
whether a long journey by raft through swampy forests, following endless, often unutterably slow columns in unexplored
bush country or even a sudden sandstorm in the dessert or a dangerous ambush.

The only possibility of spanning vast distances is the wireless.
It is everywhere, at a cartographic surveying station as well as a mobile radio unit in Chad.

The aerial in Abéché in Chad.

A German surveying unit in the Cameroons.

While the Prince of Whales is admiring a black dancer adorned with bangles at Freetown, many a puritanical lady is shocked at the innocent nudity of Sudanese beauties.

The unimaginable! Prince Arini, the son of a former cannibal king from Dahomey and a formerly notorious rebel, promenades publicly with his spouse, a Frenchwoman. He became a civil servant in Bordeaux.

Looking at the strolling beauties of Libreville, one is reminded of the Parisian Champs-Elysées.

*Her Royal Highness, the Duchess of Aosta, née Hélène of France, in a dugout on the River Buzi.
The "Beduin Princess" was always – as the legend goes – surrounded by her "black comrades in adventure".*

THE EUROPEANS ARRIVE

Once they had embarked on the great adventure of the black continent in search of new lands, civilian and military explorers alike did great deeds.

They penetrated deep into deserts, often at a great peril, where the winds lashed the sand. They reached rocky highlands cut into by fertile valleys in which black Africans planted millet, rice and vegetables. And when enough grazing lands were available, they bred animals, primarily horses, asses, cattle, sheep and goats. Often they travelled for days on end without encountering any sign of human life. And then there was the daily battle for survival, for which the native trackers proved invaluable. They could, for instance, tell from certain plants whether a waterhole was near. Where game was plentiful, menus were planned accordingly and one finds such fanciful dishes as cold guinea hen in mayonnaise or crocodile in white sauce as well as haunch of antilope or grilled boa steak.

Hunting was generally good and the "firestick" performed miracles in the incredulous eyes of the natives. A single bullet put an end to the cheerful frolicking of a hippopotamus in the water.

Three or four hours after it had gone under in a great water-spout, the powerful body re-emerged from the depths. What luck for the natives! That meant meat for a month and an indestructible all-purpose hide.

But hunting for food was not always so easy. It was, indeed, often a risky enterprise. A wounded rhino or an elephant which had been shot at but not killed was extremely dangerous. What could be worse than such raging "three or four tonners"?

When food supplies had been replenished, the expedition went on its way to bargain at one stop, to hunt at the next, everywhere flying its own banner. But no one had time for the magnificent scenery encountered on the march.

Then it was time to divide the spoils. Maps were spread out, but it was extremely difficult to draw just and reasonable boundaries between the different spheres of influence. Dangerous tensions arose between London, Paris and Berlin. Eventually reason prevailed and binding treaties were concluded.

Now diplomats followed on the heels of the explorers. Empires were born.

The steamengine in the land of the rhinoceros. Natural power is replaced by mechanical on the Brazzaville to Congo Railway. This is a urgent necessity. Stanley said that "without a railway the Congo was worthless". →

TECHNOLOGY
AND SUPERSTITION

Diplomats in Berlin and Bern have divided Africa up among the Europeans at the negotiating table.
But a great task remains: The boundaries must be drawn.
On the right bank of the Ubangi a French officer focuses his prismatic astrolabe.

The Frenchmen Périquet and the German von Ramsay meet in Magumba in a Congolese hut
"to draw up a final settlement of the entire border".

*After the agreements have been ratified, which they sign with exquisite courtesy,
it is finally possible to draw a "definitive" map of this region of Africa.*

114

An entire continent is transformed into a vast construction site which would have been worthy of the building of the Py-
ramids. At that time force was usually necessary to get most tribes to dig canals and build dams.

Millions of tonnes of earth and mud are moved by human hand.
Men work on rafts or waist-deep in mud to chop down forests or dig canals.

All these projects required enormous quantities of wood. Trees are felled and the trunks shipped into shape on the Ivory Coast. They are sent by water to construction sites, were they are made into huge railway sleepers.

The revenge of progress.
Marvellous native bridges made of lianas follow the railway bridges, which are often destroyed by the natives.

Europe's assault is halted again and again by acts of sabotage. By tearing up railway sleepers, felling trees across the lines and other such subterfuges the natives (here on the Ivory Coast, on the Abidijan-Dimbokro Railway) attempt to turn back the clocks.

The epilogue to a Senegalese drama.

The murderer of a young civil servant is executed by his own brother-in-law.
According to local custom he cuts off the head and an arm and presents them to the Colonial Administrator.

Colonel Moll is one of the many "colonial heroes".
He was killed in 1910 during the "pacification" of the Chad Ouadai.

The skeleton of the explorer Behagle. In 1899 he was murdered by Rabah,
a tyrant, who was rampaging the area of Ouadai.

Guards on a bivouac of French colonial troops, who continued to pursue "the pacification of the Chad" after Colonel Moll's death.

A classic victory. The vanquished lay their weapons at the feet of the victors.

French officialdom triumphant.
The Colonial Minister, Milliès-Lacroix, has himself borne in state through Dahomey in a sedan chair.

Young native women dance under flags symbolizing the return to peace.

TECHNOLOGY AND SUPERSTITION

The Approaches

Black Africa overflowed with natural resources like gold, ivory, rubber and timber. At first these were exploited only on a small scale. Even ostrich feathers still brought profits.

The vast expanse of land caused enormous difficulties. And the heavy surf on the rocky coasts barred trading ships from sailing directly into coastal harbours. These deserts in both north and south hindered penetration into the interior of the continent. The rivers were not navigable eight months of the year because of rapids. One had to wait for high water to travel up or down river.

After 1900 national loans in Europe made huge construction projects possible. The railway penetrated to unknown regions. Along it fields were planted and herds grazed. Schools were founded at the same time to take up the fight against native illiteracy.

The Projects

It was always impossible to solve the problem of recrui-

ting labour. In some places the railway ran through almost uninhabited regions; in others its construction caused the inhabitants to flee into the bush. This disturbed the natural demographic balance and led to acts of aggression between villages.

A new Tower of Babel arose. The construction sites brought thousands of labourers together from different tribes. They had different customs and traditions, languages and religions. It was almost impossible to keep any semblance of order. Since all travel was extremely arduous, epidemics (dysentery, pneumonia, etc.) spread among the construction crews.

Projects had to be interrupted again and again. This loss of man hours caused costs to soar beyond budget estimates, which led to new delays. The toll of human life was among the most deplorable losses. The construction of the railway between Matadi and Kinshasa may be taken as a tragic instance. Although it was built on relatively accessible terrain, it cost "per kilometre the life of an European and per sleeper the life of a black African".

The war spreads from Europe to Africa.
For the first time whites commanding blacks fight against whites commanding other blacks.
Instead of fighting against each other, the ancient tribes learn to fight in the service of foreign nations. →

AFRICA
IN THE GREAT WAR

First of all the recruiting officer must convince potential recruits tha

As soon as they get to the front the natives solve the problem of quarters in their own way. They build curious clay dwellings in odd corners of encampments.

...ey have nothing to lose and stand everything to gain if they join up.

And they discover progress in the "unseen voice" of the grammophone.

140

From spear to rifle, from the loose file to the rigid posture of the kneeling sharpshooter:
Natives learn discipline and ballistics. What they never lose is their remarkable skill in handling weapons.

Rigorous training, the hallmark of the German armed forces, works wonders with these former bush warriors, even after the silent field telephone has replaced the jungle drums.

Whether he is rigid at the head of his troops on a mule or instructing his recruits in the basics of strategy,
in the eyes of provisionary troops the officer in uniform has succeeded to the status of a "great chieftain".

From now on the combat forces decimate each other with heavy artillery fire. On the one side the German field howitzers, on the other the famed French "ninety-fives", which succeed in breaking the last resistance of troops in the Cameroons by March 1915.

A show of true loyalty on the Ivory Coast.
Two children represent in a tableau the famous placard by Poulbot, "The Recruit's Life".

From Dakkar to Mombasa many an extraordinary "flower" is growing from the Veld:
the helmets of German, English an French colonial troops.

Under a picture of the franc, a priest of Bonduka renders his tribute to the French Colonial Administration.

Life triumphs over death. Will this boy, who has been set by his proud parents on the muzzle of a cannon, really undergo a baptism of fire one day? Only the god of war can know.

A pathetic-looking German fortified Nissen hut; yet the allied troops have great difficulties in overrunning it.

A heap of corrugated metal and sacking: the foxholes of German snipers.
They laid an ambush but were forced to retreat by French artillery fire.

Strange naked squares appear suddenly in bush country: Africa's first aerodromes.

Constructing them is child's play: a few tents under a palm are all that is needed. This German doubledecker has arrived too late for the war effort.

Dr. Seitz

From the portable typewriter of an allied war correspondent, the news goes round the world. After a glorious fight Dr. Seitz, Commander of the German troops in Southwest Africa, has surrendered. The war in this part of the world ends with a chivalrous gesture. The visitor, General Louis Botha, extends his hand to his unfortunate adversary.

On the entry of the allied troops who have defeated the Germans, various tribes pay hommage to their "liberators".
The old order has changed, but they too are intruders.

Wreathed in smile these sharpshooters return by net to a pacified earth.

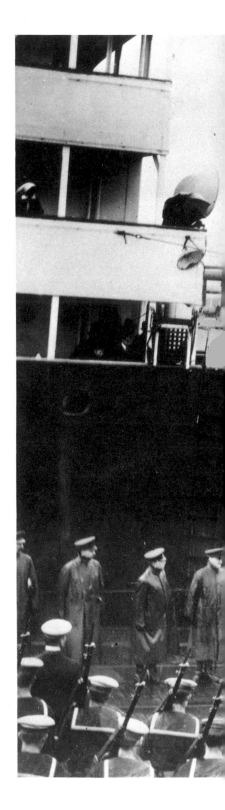

The triumphant return to Cape Town of the South African General Botha. During the Boer Wars the enemy of the English, he has made peace in the name of the Crown for the formerly German colony of Southwest Africa.

Senegalese during victory celebrations. This marks the beginning of a new Africa, an Africa which has spilled its blood for Europe.

AFRICA IN THE GREAT WAR

In 1880 Germany had no overseas colonies. In 1914 Germans governed a farflug colonial empire. In 1918 Germany went back to square one. It had lost all its overseas possessions.

First Togo was given up. The general Louis Botha conquered all of West Africa. The Cameroons fell to British, French and Belgian troops. After valiant resistance German East Africa was put under allied rule.

The Fall of the Cameroons

In 1913 the Cameroons seemed to have the best prospects of all German colonies. This rich region was of great strategic significance as well.

Immediately hostilities had begun on 5th August 1914, England and France prepared to overrun it. Following a sea blockade of the Cameroons and after its 4150 km of border had been encircled, its main trouble spots were assaulted at once.

This strategy forced the German troops to split up. Finally one base after another had to surrender to overwhelming enemy forces and by the end of 1915 the allies had taken over the Cameroons.

The Black Army

France's black army, which had continued to grow in strength since the beginning of the century, contributed substantially to this victory.

Since 1900 the Europeans had been mobilizing natives after noticing that putting them into uniform taught men discipline.

Most of these provisionary soldiers were former slaves. They were enthusiastic, not only about the pay received after four years as auxiliaries; they were also overjoyed at the prospect of good food and lodging. They particularly liked the splendid colourful uniforms topped by the chéchia, the red beret of the French colonial soldiers.

The Senegalese were particularly valiant soldiers. Unlike most of their companions in arms, they bore changes in climate without ill effects on their martial virtue. They tended to become professional very quickly since most of them joined up again after their first term of service.

The Senegalese regiments, which went into the field accompanied by wives and children, were a pitoresque sight indeed. That was not a bad thing. On the contrary, if the Senegalese soldier discharged his duty admirable in the field, his wife was a valuable companion on the march. She prepared rice and couscous, not only for her husband, but for his unmarried comrades. Families could thus remain together.

Two civilizations confront each other.
The tracked vehicles of the expedition organized by André Citroen in 1924 meet riders armed with laces by Lake Chad.
After the war "the modern adventurers" no longer dream of conquering the world; they merely want to tame the wilds. →

FROM TRACK
TO ROAD

An unexpected flirt at an elephant cemetery.
G.M. Haardt, one of those responsible for the Citroen expedition, meets a charming native.

His meeting with the "Beduine Princess", HéLène of France, Duchess of Aosta, is, on the other hand, very formal.

These charming moments should not let us forget the enormous obstacles against which tracked vehicles had to struggle in the mire of the Wadis.

In the course of the journey the difficulties grew worse and the fords deeper.
In order to cross Lake Nyasa the generator had to be dismantled and the vehicles had to be towed.

Sometimes it is possible to construct a temporary bridge over a small river.
But at other times, as here, crossing Lake Kenia in Ubangi-Shari, the expedition has to improve a ferry from dugouts lashed together.

At each halt the expedition leaders confer with each other.
Above, from left to right, Major Bettembourg, G.M. Haardt and Louis Audouin-Dubreuil.

Problems galore. Elephants and giraffes are hunted to feed the columns of bearers who carry the expedition's fuel.
This does not prevent Jacoleff, the expedition's artist, from making a quick sketch of a giraffe before dinner.

"Reached the Indian Ocean today, 14th June 1925 at Mozambique, the point on the African continent closest to Madagascar." Haardt sent this triumphant wire to André Citroen. The expedition had taken eight months.

One of the two hydroplanes of Sub-Lieutenants Bernard and Guilbaud on the Niger. Crossed and re-crossed in all directions by car and now by hydroplane, mysterious Africa is soon to become a land in which all Europe will begin building.

For aviators the time of peaceful missions has come.
During a scientific expedition through Africa, Blériot's four-engine plane "Roland Garros" has a stopover in Tessalit

FROM TRACK TO ROAD

The great war was over and with it the rivalry between scientists and military expeditions. It was an era of peaceful conquest to open up inaccessible areas by means of new land and air routes.

In February 1920 Major Vuillemin became the first man to cross the Sahara by air. He was followed by the motor expedition of Haardt and Audoin-Dubreuil from Tougourt to Timbuktu (17th December 1922 to 7th January 1923).

The conditions under which these expeditions took place beggar description.

Between 5th December 1924 and 26th February 1925, the two journalists Train and Duverne crossed Africa alone by car from east to west, from Conakry to the Red Sea. They passed through wide stretches of country without roads, beset by natural obstacles like deserts, swamps and mountains. The plain of Cameroon was flooded so they only made sixty kilometres in nine days. Wherever they were overtaken by flooding they took the electrical wiring out of the car and had the generator, sparkplugs and battery carried on their native bearers' heads while the car was towed through the water. In Fort Lamy they met Captain Delingette, accompanied by his wife and a mechanic, who had set out in November 1921 on a journey of 23,000kms from Béchar to the Cape.

But the most important event of that time was without doubt the Citroen Expedition.

On 28th October 1924 the Convoy of eight tracked vehicles set out from Béchar. In Kampala (Uganda) they split up on 15th April 1925 into four groups. Three of them were to meet again at Majunga on the west coast of Madagascar and to reach Tananarive until 8th September 1925.

SOUTH AFRICA

In Transvaal the Boers still wear the serve habit of their Calvinistic forbears, who came from Holland in the 17th century. True to tradition, the father of a clan, at once judge, pastor and patriarch, still rules over his numerous progeny.

THE LAND OF THE
BOERS

The Boers, cattle breeders and farmers, use such cars principally to carry food and supplies.

*An earthly paradise in Transvaal is the valley of French Hoeg. 200
French Huguenots settled here after the Edict of Nantes was revoked by Louis XIV.*

Cowboys take a coffee break.

In 1886 gold is discovered in Transvaal.
The sand dumped after sifting to a high plateau.

This raw diamond weighs 3024 carats.
It was found near Pretoria.

This diamond mine near Kimberley is one of the greatest pits ever excavated.

Mounted police in Johannesburg.
The influx of foreigners, particularly the English, makes the gold capital look like a frontier town in America's Wild West.

The high street of Ladysmith in Natal has not yet been paved.

Pretoria, the capital of Transvaal, is still a small town of 15,000 inhabitants.

The market in Kimberley, Bechuanaland. Each morning the Boers from the countryside bring their produce into town.

The executive council of the Republic of Transvaal in Pretoria. In the middle is Paul Kruger,
cted President in 1833. He is flanked by his future generals: on the left Joubert, on the right Cronje.

Her subservient manner, her homely virtues and her piety make Mme. Kruger the ideal Boer wife.

President Kruger.

All classes travel together in the coal carriage to make the 1650 km journey from the Cape to Johannesburg in 70 hours.

THE LAND OF THE BOERS

The Republic of Transvaal was founded by the Boers. They are the descendants of Dutch families and French Huguenots who were driven out of France after Louis XIV. revoke the Edict of Nantes. They were farmers who rejected the Anglo-Saxon way of life. After the 17th century, when they settled in the Cape area, they continued to withdraw further into the hinterland before the encroaching English. On their way north they founded first the Republic of Natal, which was annexed by Britain in 1883, then the Orange Free State, which was occupied by the British in 1848, but afterwards liberated, and finally the Republic of Transvaal.

In 1877 Britain was anxious to annex Transvaal after the battles against the Zulu King Cetewayo. The Boers however rebelled against this abuse of power and proclaimed the independence of the Republic of Transvaal. Under Kruger, Joubert and Pretorius they withdrew, armed to the teeth, to the borders of Natal. The British were defeated in 1881 and recognized the Boer Free State as a sovereign state.

The Boers paid dearly for their Victory. Trade and commerce broke down and the population was discouraged.

Since 1886 the discovery of gold has changed the country completely. Everywhere new cities were growing up and capital and immigrants poured into the country. The national budget showed a large surplus.

The two most Important Cities in Transvaal in 1898

The capital, Pretoria, was named after the first President, Pretorius, elected in 1848. It was the seat of government under Kruger. There were no large buildings in this settlement of 12,000 inhabitants.

The discovery of gold in 1886 led to a great influx of foreigners. Mining camps shot up everywhere. One of the largest of these was called Johannesburg in honour of President Kuger and General Joubert, both of whom were named Johannes. The city grew by leaps and bounds. In 1886 it consisted of only one thoroughfare, but in June 1887, it sheltered 14,000 goldhunters. An exchange and four churches were built and houses sprang up everywhere.

By the end of November there were over 68 mining companies. Johannesburg became the commercial metropolis of South Africa.

In October 1899 the war between Transvaal and the Orange Free State against Britain began. The Boers, farmer soldiers without uniforms, were dreaded marksmen. →

193

FARMER SOLDIERS

Hans Lemmen.

Hans Botha (70 years old).

D. Roos.

Hans Enasimus.
Former generals of the Boer army went back into active service. They dressed no differently from their men.

General Joubert, the Commander-in-Chief of the Transvaal forces, enjoys with his men a meal cooked by his wife.

Young officers who are, once more, to play a great part:
General de Wet, the Artful Dodger.

ouis Botha, the future Commander-in-Chief.

Mejer.

Smuts, one of the signers of the Versailles Treaty.

Aged 65, 15 and 43: Three generations of Boers.
All eligible men, 55,000 in all, were called up.

A guard post near Ladysmith.

Like guerillas the Boers are adept at exploiting the advantages of the terrain.

"Long Tom", one of the most illustrious Boer cannons,
leaves Pretoria amid great cheering to go to the aid of the men fighting at Ladysmith.

A unit files through the "Veld" near Newcastle in Natal. Mobility assured the Boer army impressive victories.

With the aid of a splendid team of oxen, the convoy finally reaches Ladysmith despite bad roads and missing bridges.

"Long Tom's" journey.

A 155mm gun manufactured by the French Creusot Works is deployed before Ladysmith.

With his field glass this Boer soldier shows his men how to aim a small cannon more accurately.

er cities in Transvaal and the Orange Free State were fortified like Mafeking.

The commissariat follows.

To show their enthusiasm for the cause of the Boers many Europeans enlist in the Transvaal forces. General L. Botha, the French Lieutenant Gallopard and the Italian Captain Ricchiardi share a tent.

The French volunteers are commanded by Lieutenant Gallopard.

Native trackers help Lieutenant Gallopard.

Italian volunteers with their commander, Captain Ricchiardi.

Dutch volunteers unfurl their standard.

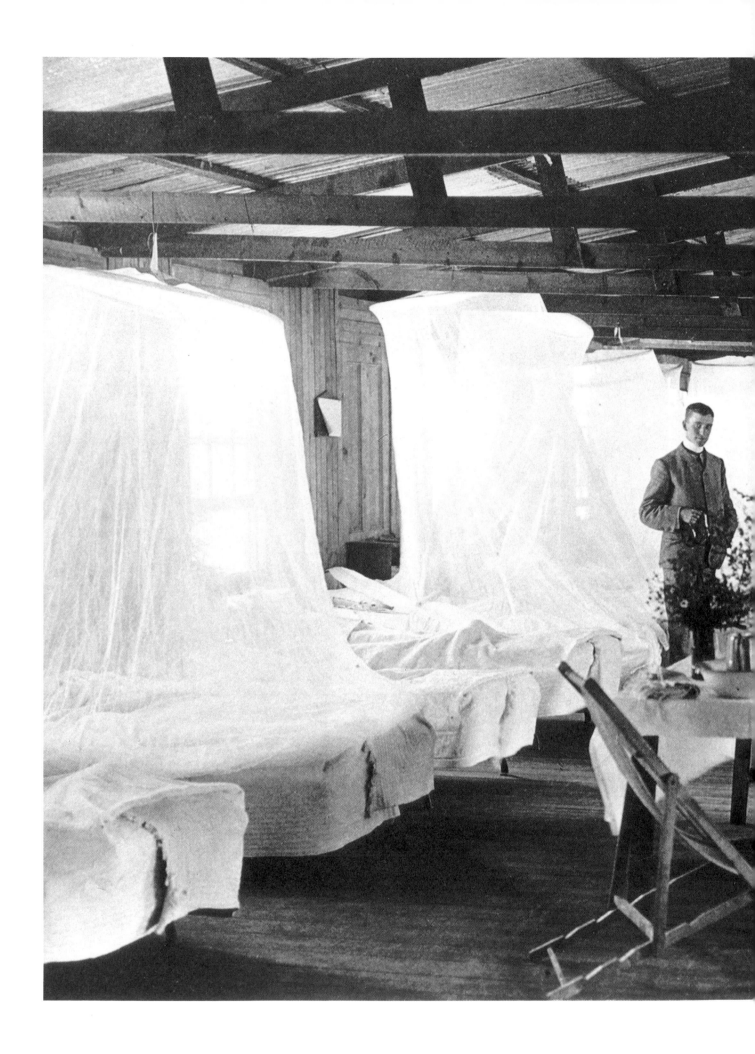

Hostilities can begin. Even the hospital beds are ready.

Boers enjoy the last few hours of peace in a field camp.

FARMER SOLDIERS

Jameson's attack

Late in December 1895 Dr. Jameson, High Commissioner of Matabele and Mashonaland, left his territory with armed troops and attacked Transvaal.

Jameson acted under orders from the powerful "British South Africa Company". This company, whose director was Cecile Rhodes, had control of great expanse of land between the Orange River and Lake Tanganyika. Now it was anxious to annex Transvaal too in order to gain possession of the rich goldfields.

Dr. Jameson's undertaking was defeated by strong resistance. But it was a taste of what was to come in 1899.

War

In this war the Boers fought for freedom and independence. The British fought for possession of the vast rich country. It was not so much a war against the Republic of South Africa as a conflict between Britain and South Africa. The white population was composed of Dutch, German, French and English settlers. They lived not only in Transvaal and the Orange Free State but also in the Cape Colony and Natal. South Africa was whole-heartedly on the side of Transvaal.

The British troops were stationed between Ladysmith, Dundee, Newcastle and Charlestown. They were noticeably inferior in numbers to the Transvaal forces, where, because every Boer took up arms in time of war, an army of 55,000 men could be called up.

The British and Boer Armies

Two different strategies confronted each other. The British army fought by marching up to the enemy and defending its batteries to the bitter end. The Boer soldiers, on the other hand, stole up, hid and were willing to yield terrain if necessary. They wanted to kill without risking loss of life.

In the first months of the war the Boers had a definitive edge. They besieged the most important British bases, particularly Ladysmith.

However, they soon slowed to a standstill. Confronted by the British troops, for whom replacements poured in steadily after 1900, they were soon discouraged.

The Johannesburg detachment – comprising all Boers able to bear arms in the district – files out of Botha's Pass over the dry "Veld" to re-assemble at Newcastle in Natal in October 1899. →

WAR IN TRANSVAAL

From 1900 on the well-disciplined British troops regularly defeat the extremely mobile and valiant Boer fighters.

Cecile Rhodes.

In the presence of the representatives of Her Majesty, Lords Roberts and Kitchener,
the British flag is raised on the square before the City Hall at Johannesburg. The Boers were forced to abandon their
cities one by one, the capital Pretoria and Johannesburg, and to retreat to the plains.

The victory of the British over the Boers is above all due to the numerical superiority of an army which is steadily receiving replacements.

The British forces receive support from the entire Empire, as here from Canadian scouts.

But even for the British the war is no pushover.
After each battle, sharply observed by the General Staffs of both sides, many dead are left on the field.

With their artillery the Boers are more than the match of the British.
Mortars, 155mm shells and howitzers take their toll of the British ranks.

231

The spoils of war. The freight of this British train loaded with artillery pieces in Pretoria Station will considerably strengthen the firepower of the British forces.

The British live in continual fear of Boer inroads on their munitions and supply trains.
The British convoy can be raided by Boers at any time.

Immediately after such stealthy and devastating raids the farmer soldiers withdraw to their territory.

The cruel face of dead on the battlefield.

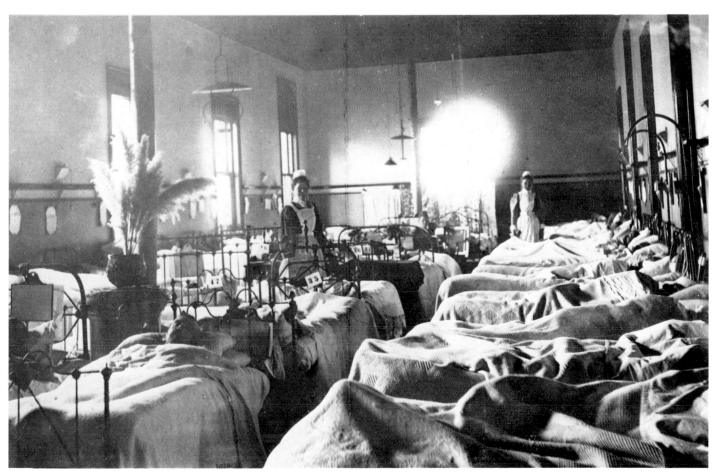

The International Red Cross cares for the wounded: Russian ambulances, Dutch doctors.
Volunteers pour into Boer field hospitals from all over the world to help the men who have come through yet again.

Huge internment camps receive British prisoners of war. Towards the end of the war there are so many prisoners that the Boers cannot accommodate any more. They simply strip the British soldier of their uniforms and drive them out into the bush.

A time-honoured British tactic. The captured Boers are exiled to the island of St Helena.

244

A funeral is a solemn moment for the Boers. A dead man means one fighter less. There are no replacements.
Due to the lack of reserves the Boer forces are becoming fatally weakened. This is the ultimate cause of their defeat.

Once the Boers laid siege to the British settlements of Ladysmith and Kimberley. Now they no longer have enough supplies to retake cities of their own occupied by the British. They spread out over the plains with arms and baggage.

WAR IN TRANSVAAL

The Boers triumphed at first due to their great mobility. From 1900 on, however, the war changed completely in the face of the superbly equipped and well-disciplined British army.

The British liberated Kimberley and went on to overrun the Orange Free State and to occupy Johannesburg and Pretoria. The Boers did not even bother to defend the two cities since they rather were guerilleros than soldiers. President Kruger retreated to the north. He wanted to prolong the war by all means as long as possible.

The Government Retreats

The government of the Republic of Transvaal became mobile. It had its seat in a railway carriage which usually stood in a station 180 kilometres from Pretoria. In August 1900 President Kruger announced:

"It is true that the capital has fallen. But now the capital of the Republic, the seat of the government, is here, in this railway carriage. Our country is occupied; but the civil government is still able to perform its duties. This railway carriage which I have built to take me anywhere at any time my presence is needed will bring me back to Pretoria."

Near the railway station a provisional capital grew up. The President's staff lived in tents. The British occupation of Pretoria was by no means the end of the war. To the contrary, the Boer leaders had become virtually unassailable and harassed the enemy troops more than ever.

Until 1902 skirmishes were fought daily all over the Republic of Transvaal and the Orange Free State and even occasionally on the territory of the Cape Colony.

Things were at a stalemate. The war refused to end and the heroic days when the English preferred death to surrender were a thing of the past. In order to put more pressure on the Boers they went so far as to intern women and children in concentration camps. A journalist sent the following cable to his paper:

"... The internment camps in which so many innocent, defenceless victims are held captive by soldiers whilst their farms burn on the horizon, blown up by dynamite, will ultimately be self-destructive. Women mutter curses, boys brandish threatening fists and dream of revenge. All these pitiful beings, who have been herded together in the camps like wretched cattle, where they vegetate for weeks on end without bread, wracked with fever, without a doctor's care, without medicaments – these pictures of horror will linger long in the mind's eye and the memory will be for England one source of irredeemable injustice."

A figure of legend. The English Colonel, Baden-Powell, the hero of Mafeking when it was under siege by the Boers, is inspired by his military experiences to found a peace corps, which the majority of his country's youth join: the Scouts. →

THE BIRTH OF A NATION

In top hat and frock Johannes Kruger, the Boer President and former cattle farmer, goes on land at Marseille.
Things are looking grim at Transvaal. He is seeking help in Europe, but is fobbed off with mere declarations of sympathy
for his country's plight, where meanwhile his companions in arms are drawing up a peace treaty.

The British do not permit him to return.
He will never see his native land, where his wife has died, again.
He dies in Europe but is interred in 1904 with great ceremony in Pretoria.

251

The war is at an end.
A new life begins in Transvaal, in Johannesburg and in Pretoria, where the peace treaty is signed.
South Africa has become a British dominion and elects its own parliament,
which is opened in Cape Town in 1910 in the presence of the Duke of Connaught, an uncle of the British King.
As a gesture of conciliation, a pastor of the Reformed Dutch Church is allowed to read the prayers.

In 1918 the South Africans helped the allies on the French front to defeat the German army.

Now they may take part in negotiations for peace at Versailles.
Their reward is a mandate over the former German colonies in West Africa.

The Boers were shepherds both before and after the war.
A modern Cincinnatus, General de Wet, supervises shearing on his farm near Pretoria.

THE BIRTH OF A NATION

Peace

On 31st May 1902 the peace treaty was signed at Pretoria which in all points was in Britain's favour. Yet for the Boers not all was lost, for they gained recognition from the victors. Four years later they obtained the right of self-government and Louis Botha, the former Commander-in-Chief, became Prime Minister.

The South African Union

In 1910 the Duke of Connaught, an uncle of the British King, opened the first parliament of the South African Union. Because he was presenting the world with its third federal republic under British dominion after Canada and Australia, he was performing an act of great political significance.

"The United States of South Africa", the dream of both Cecile Rhodes and Kruger, was achieved in the union of the five South African colonies: The Cape of Good Hope, Natal, Transvaal, the Orange Free State and Rhodesia. Nevertheless it was an uneasy union, for, of the six million inhabitants of the country, 1.25 million where white, mainly of Dutch descent, and the rest were members of diverse native races.

This imbalance could well one day – as the future was to show – bring serious problems and severe conflicts.

The Great War

In 1915 General Louis Botha annexed German South-west Africa in the name of Britain.

Since South Africa had also fought for the allies on the French front, the Boer generals Botha and Smuths were entitled to share in drawing up the Treaty of Versailles. They defended the interests of the South African Union, which demanded the right to administer the former German colonies. In this they were successful.

INDEX

THE DISCOVERY AND DIVISION OF AFRICA

Portuguese Voyages of Discovery along the Coast

1416 Cape Bojador (today Mauretania) is reached.
1445 Discovery of Cape Verde.
1471 The Equator is crossed.
1482 Discovery of the Mouth of the Congo.
1487 Bartholomew Diaz sails round the Cape of Storms (later the Cape of Good Hope).
1498 Vasco da Gama sails round the Cape and up the East Coast of Africa on his way to India.

The Most Important Discoveries on Land

1482 The Frenchman René Caillié is the first Christian to reach Timbuktu.
1848–1894 The Germans Kraf and Rebmann discover the volcanos of Mt Kilimanjaro and Mt Kenia.
1849 The Scottish missionary David Livingstone (1813–1873) reaches the Zambezi.
1852–1854 Livingstone crosses the continent from Zambezi to Luanda.
1856 Livingstone discovers Victoria Falls on the Zambezi.
1856–1858 The German Barth explores the region of Lake Chad.
1857–1859 The Englishmen Burton and Speke discover Lakes Tanganyika and Victoria.
1858–1864 Livingstone discovers Lake Nyasa and the Rovuma.
1860–1863 Speke and Grant prove that Lake Victoria is the main source of the Nile.
1861 Burton explores Mt Cameroon.
1863–1865 The Englishman Baker proves that Lake Albert is also a source of the Nile.
1863–1866 The French Mage reaches the Niger in Ségou from Senegal.
1864–1866 Livingstone sets out from Lake Tanganyika and unknowingly comes upon the upper reaches of the Congo. He meets Stanley in 1871 at Udjidji.
1869–1873 Henry Morton Stanley (1841–1904) leads an expedition from Zanzibar to lake Tanganyika.

1873–1876 The Englishman Cameron crosses Africa from east to west at the Equator.
1874 Stanley explores the course of the Lualaba (Congo).
1876–1878 The Frenchman Pierre Savorgnan de Brazza (1852–1905) explores Gaboon and the course of the Ogooué.
1876–1879 Portuguese expedition under Serpa Pinto de Benguela to Durban.
1879–1884 In the service of the Belgian King, Leopold II, Stanley explores the course of the Congo and finds its source in 1877.
1879–1885 Brazza explores the right bank of the Congo, which he takes possession of for France.
1844–1899 The German Carl Peters explores the basin of the Zambezi.
1896–1898 Captain Marchand unites Chad with Djibuti. His mission ends at Fashoda on the Upper Nile.
1900 The expedition of Gentil, Forreau and Lamy as well as Joulland meet at the Mountain of the Logone at the future site of Fort Lamy.

The Main Stages of the Division of Africa

The situation in 1880: European possessions are limited to a strip of coast.

GREAT BRITAIN	FRANCE	PORTUGAL
Gambia (1765)	Senegal (1783-1815) Administration implemented by Faidherbe (1854-1863)	Angola
The Cape Territory (1806-1814)		Mozambique (command posts since the 16th century)
Sierra Leone (1807)		
Aden (1839)	The Ivory Coast (1843)	
The Gold Coast (1843)	Guinea and Gaboon (1843-1844)	
Natal (1845)		
Lagos (1861)		
Behuanaland (1879-1885)		

1880–1914 The fight for Africa.
1880–1898 The conquest of the western Sudan by France in 1882.

● Great Britain occupies Egypt (protectorate 1914) and the Sudan.
● Mahdist revolt in the Sudan.
● France annexes the Congo (Brazzaville in 1884).
● Great Britain recognizes Portuguese claims in Cabinda.
● Creation of British Somalia.
● The three German colonies are founded: Southwest Africa, the Cameroons and Togo.
1884–1885 The Berlin Congress on the Congo establishes regulations for taking possession of colonies and creates a neutral Congo under the sovereignty of Leopold II of Belgium (who turns it over to Belgium in 1908).
1885 German East Africa is founded.
1886 British-German treaty on the division of East Africa.
1888–1891 British Rhodesia is founded.
1890 British-German treaty: The German Empire regains Helgoland in exchange for Zanzibar and Uganda.
1895–1896 France annexes Madagascar.
1898 British-German treaty on the Portuguese colonies. Crisis at Fashoda between Great Britain and France.
1899 After it has been reconquered by Kitchener the Sudan becomes an Anglo-Egyptian Condominium. The Anglo-Portuguese Treaty of Windsor: Great Britain guarantees the existence of the Portuguese colonies.
1899–1902 The Boer War.
1904 The creation of the Gouvernement Générale of French West Africa (l'Afrique Occidentale Française – A.O.F.) which includes Mauretania, Senegal, the Sudan, Dahomey and Niger. The Anglo-French Entente and the settlement of colonial issues under dispute.
1910 The creation of the Gouvernement Général of French Equatorial Africa (l'Afrique Equatoriale Française – A.E.F.), which includes Chad, Ubangi-Shari, Gaboon and the French Congo. The Union of South Africa is created.
1911 German-French treaty on Marocco and the Congo.

1919 The Division of the German Colonies

GREAT BRITAIN	FRANCE	BELGIUM	UNION OF SOUTH AFRICA
Tanganyika Part of the Cameroons Western Togo	Eastern Togo Part of the Cameroons	Ruanda-Urundi	Southwest Africa

THE BOER WAR

1806–1814 Great Britain annexes the Cape Colony.
1836–1844 The "Great Trek": The Boers retreat into the hinterlands.
1842 The Orange Free State is founded.
1853 The South African Republic of Transvaal is founded.
1867 Diamonds are found at Kimberley. Great Britain annexes Griqualand despite the claim of the Orange Free State.
1877–1888 First Boer War. The British are defeated at Majuba Hill and must renounce all claim to Transvaal.
1881–1884 The Convention of Pretoria: Great Britain recognizes the independence of Transvaal.
1890–1896 Paul Kruger is elected President of Transvaal.
1886 Gold is found in Transvaal.
1890–1896 The Prime Minister of the Cape Territory, Cecile Rhodes, prepares to invade the Boer Republics.
1895 The Jameson attack on Transvaal fails.
Oct. 1899 Hostilities begin.
Oct.–Dec. 1899 Boer victories (Sieges of Ladysmith, Mafeking, Kimberley).
Feb. 1900 British counteroffensive.
March 1900 The British enter Bloemfontein, Johannesburg and Pretoria.
Dec. 1900 Kruger travels to Europe.
1900–1902 The Boer guerilla war.
31st May 1902 The Treaty of Pretoria: Transvaal and the Orange Free State become two Crown Colonies.
31st May 1910 The Union of South Africa is founded.

© JEUNESSE VERLAGSANSTALT/ VADUZ
UND
© SWAN PRODUCTIONS AG, ZUG/SWITZERLAND

ISBN 3–89434–006–1

ART DIRECTOR: CLAUDE SIRE
ICONOGRAPHY: BASCHET & CIE
PRINTED IN WEST GERMANY ON THE PRESSES OF
DRUCKEREI UHL, RADOLFZELL

OKTOBER 1989

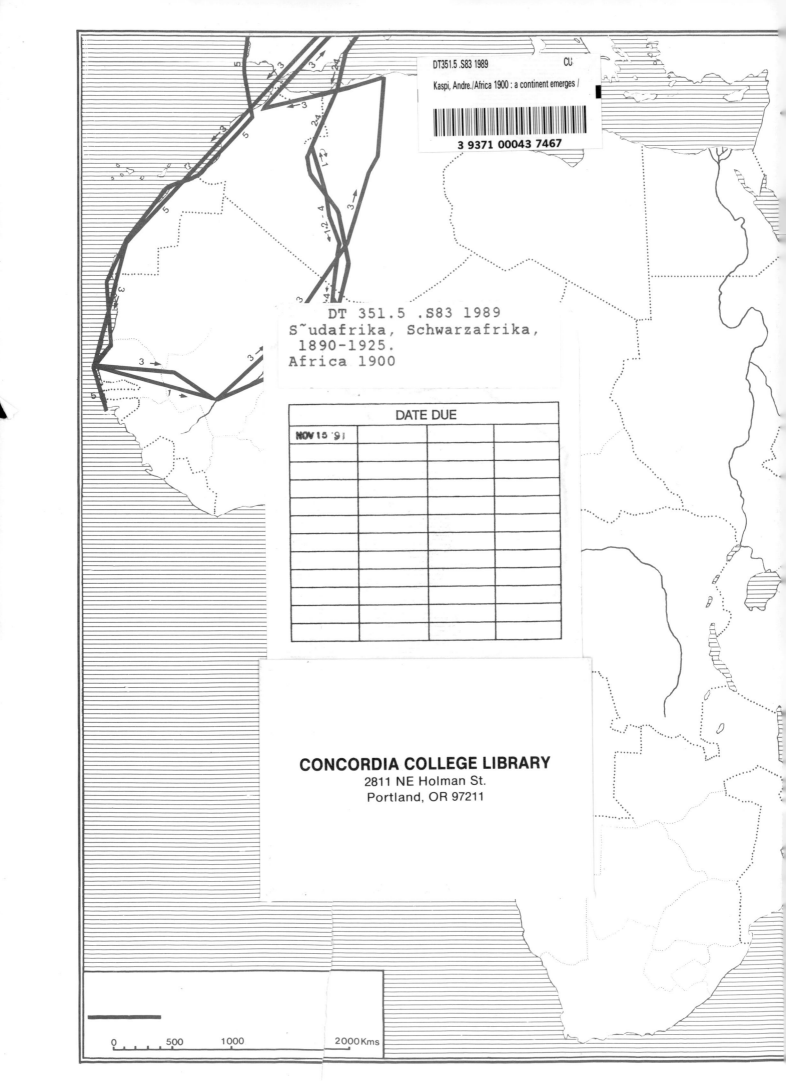

0   500   1000   2000 Kms